GROWTH HAC

Innovative Marketing Tactics to Grow Faster and Smarter

BOOK DESCRIPTION

The emergence of Web and Mobile technologies have revolutionalized the way businesses are conducted. Those enterprises that have leveraged these technologies have made tremendous exponential growth. Google, Facebook, Uber, Dropbox, Twitter, Amazon, are just but a few examples of those enterprises that leveraged these technologies to reap big rewards.

This book is about sharing with you innovative marketing tactics to grow faster and smarter. The book does not assume your level of knowledge and understanding of what Growth Hacking is all about. Thus, it starts with a beginner's approach by introducing you to what growth hacking is all about and builds upon this foundation to guide you into a more detailed perspectives.

Knowledge without application is redundant. This book gives you practical hands-on techniques on how you should apply growth hacking to achieve great success. These techniques touch on all stages of your brand's funnel right from customer acquisition, customer activation, customer retention, revenue generation and referral. It further provides you with growth hacking strategy that you can employ using these techniques to grow faster and smarter.

Like any business enterprise, having the right people to run it is paramount. Growth hacking is not an exception. Yet, building a team for growth hacking require a uniquely different approach than what we are accustomed to in the traditional approach. This book not only presents you with different proven models of growth team but also helps you to identify the right hackers for your team. In this regard, it provides you with tips and qualities to look for in a hacker and the key competencies required.

Growth, like a vehicle moving on a highway, requires levers (Gears) to be able to move on (be they manual or automatic). The most critical elements of growth are its levers. Failure to identify levers simply means uncertain growth. This book helps you to identify critical levers for your brand and the relevant drivers that can propel it so that you can have a more predictable growth.

Attracting customers is a critical component of growth hacking. Yet, without a great first impression, this comes to naught. From this book, you will be able to learn the best ways to attract customers through a great first impression, appropriate acquisition hacks and right engagement. Follow-ups are great. Yet inappropriate follow-ups can turn-off your existing and potential customers. You will also learn follow-up hacks that can bring forth a great impact on your targets for greater growth.

Customer retention is the most prized treasure of any marketing endeavor. Without it, you lose your customers faster than a leaking tank loses water. Through this book, you will learn customer retention hacks that help to protect your growth reservoir.

Finally, you are running a business. You need to make money. This book provides you with proven monetization hacks that you can employ to guarantee you exponential income growth that not only rewards you for your smart innovation but also assures your business future.

Enjoy reading.

GIFT INCLUDED

If you are an entrepreneur, an aspiring entrepreneur, someone who is trying to create additional income stream, or even someone who just loves self improvement books; then you need to read my recommendations for top 10 business books ever. These are book that I have read that have changed my life for the better.

Top 10 Business Books

ABOUT THE AUTHOR

George Pain is an entrepreneur, author and business consultant. He specializes in setting up online businesses from scratch, investment income strategies and global mobility solutions. He has built several businesses from the ground up, and is excited to share his knowledge with readers. Here is a list of his books.

Books of George Pain

DISCLAIMER

CONTENTS

INTRODUCTION

Hacking became a new buzz created with the advent of internet revolution. Though, initially, it had been attributed to the illegal and criminal act of gaining access to internet resources. However, as people came to appreciate the creative power behind hacking, they have applied it to great positive endeavors.

The first nuclear experience brought horror. But, over time, nuclear energy has saved the world from consequences overexploitation of scarce energy resources, saved lives through medical applications and boosted industrialization through manufacturing applications. This verily applies to hacking.

This book introduces you to growth hacking, a relatively new concept in business entrepreneurship that is focused on growth. It further provides you with innovative marketing tactics to grow faster and smarter so that you can optimize the benefits that accrue to you by leveraging the limitless possibilities of internet technology to your advantage.

Many enterprises have experienced almost miraculous exponential growth through growth hacking. The leading ecommerce giants such as Amazon and tech giants such as Google, Facebook, Twitter, Airbnb, Uber, among so many others discovered growth hacking early enough and have reaped billions of dollars out of it. You too should not be left out. This is your guide. It is time to grab your pie.

Keep reading!

WHAT IS GROWTH HACKING?

Growth hacking is an innovative approach to business in which revolutionary and disruptive technology are used to catapult growth to levels that would not be traditionally achievable.

Is growth hacking legal?

Hacking has ceased to be a term applied to the old traditional criminal activity. Hacking has metamorphosed into a terminology that means tapping into newer and innovative ways of doing things. That's why the term no longer resides in the province of computers and has extended into everyday life domains including business, health, relationships, etc. Thus, growth hacking is legal.

How does growth hacking work?

Like traditional hacking, growth hacking is about carefully studying a system of doing things, finding loopholes that make it vulnerable and exploiting those loopholes to generate new funnels.

In a better sense, we can look at the system as a tank. This tank has leaks. These leaks can be tapped as new channels/funnels of irrigating plants (business plants) so that they can be able properly watered (since water that would have otherwise gone to waste has been tapped and redirected to irrigation).

Product-market fit: The core essence of growth hacking

Growth hacking is about intelligently utilizing data metrics to device innovative ways to bridge the gap between product and market such that the product can perfectly fit the market.

Why growth hacking?

From our analogy of a leaking tank, we can see growth hacking as serving the following purposes:

- It reduces wastage – Resources that would have otherwise been wasted are converted into use. In a business perspective, this waste could be dissatisfied customers, frustrated creative workforce, poorly employed technology (e.g. ecommerce, social media, etc)

- It turns un-utilized potential into a new kinetic (growth) force – Un-utilized potential could include wastage (as seen above), unexplored potential (e.g. untapped market, unemployed creative workforce, unemployed technology, etc)

- It optimizes resource utilization – This includes converting wastage into a new source, tapping into unemployed potential and blending with existing utilization in such a manner that optimizes productivity, value-addition, customer satisfaction, and growth.

What are some of the core areas where growth hacking is applicable?

Growth hacking involves online technologies. Thus, there are diverse areas where growth hacking can be applied provided that online tools and technologies can be utilized for purposes of customer acquisition, activation, engagement, and retention.

Who is a growth hacker?

Every field has its professionals, growth hacking is no exception. The professionals in charge of growth hacking are known as growth hackers.

What does one need to be a growth hacker?

The qualities required of a growth hacker are quite different from those required for traditional business roles. There are several core competencies that one must possess to be to qualify as a growth hacker.

For more information on key competencies of a growth hacker, read section on "Building a Team of Growth".

Growth hacking – It is all in the mindset

Growth hacking requires a certain peculiar mindset for it to flourish. This mindset is reinforced by certain habitual patterns that need to be formulated and carried out for success.

Benefits of growth hacking

- Gap bridging – Growth hacking bridges the gap between product and market

- Focus – Growth hacking enables a focus on key growth drivers

- Momentum sustenance – Through repetitive acts of improvisation through customer engagement and feedback, greater momentum is sustained.

- Revenue optimization – Due to focus on growth, revenue is optimized as non-revenue generating channels are overlooked.

Key features of growth hacking

- Growth hacking focuses on targeted segment

- Growth hacking is dependant on individual creativity

- Growth hacking creates a community rather than customers

HOW SHOULD YOU APPLY GROWTH HACKING?

When should you consider growth hacking?

First and foremost, before you think of the how, you need to establish the why and when (the need arises). In this regard, you should be able to answer the following key questions:

1. When is the right time to apply growth hacking?

2. What is the most appropriate structure for your growth team?

3. Who are the key hackers in your growth team?

When is the right time to apply growth hacking?

Well, the right time to apply growth hacking is after you have been able to carry out research and analytics such that you come to establish two key things:

- A product that people love

- A need to grow this product efficiently

How is growth hacking process like?

Growth hacking process involves the following key processes;

1. Idea generation

2. Organization of idea

3. Testing of idea

4. Analyzing

5. Optimizing

6. Repeat the process

What metrics are used to determine the success of a growth hack?

There are five key metrics used to determine the success of a growth hacks. Each of these metrics is designed to test each of the 5 key growth levers – Acquisition, Activation, Retention, Revenue and Referral (AARRR). Further discussions on AARRR are found in the section titled "Indentifying Your Growth Levers", herein after.

Acquisition – How do users find you?

Metrics on acquisition help you determine how fast the targeted flow enters your channel's funnel. For example, if your acquisition channel is Organic SEO, the SEO metrics will help you determine which SEO Keywords bring more traffic and which ones bring less traffic. This will help you enhance those ones that bring more traffic through strategic repositioning (e.g. on product's page) and blending it with appropriate secondary keywords to have a better long-tail keyword for better targeting.

For more information on acquisition read the section on "Attracting Customers"

Activation – Do users have a great first experience?

Metrics on activation helps to determine whether users have a great first experience or not. This enables the activation process to be redesigned and re-engineered to remove those bottlenecks that prevent this great experience. For example, when readers land on your blog page, page metrics can help you establish how long they spend their time on that page. If reading the entire page requires 10 minutes, yet most spent only 3 minutes; that could be an indicator that, though the title is attractive, the content didn't grant them a great user experience.

For more information on activation, read the section on "First impressions", "Engage and Educate" and "Follow Up"

Retention – Do users come back?

Metrics on retention helps to determine how frequent your activations revisit/repurchase/reactivate your product. For example, let's say you have a blog or a product that ought to be consumed perpetually, and you find out that the percentage of those customers who make a repetitive action is low. This simply means that you must find out why the retention levels are low and redesign your product to boost this retention level.

For more information on retention, read the section on "Customer retention".

Revenue – How do you make money?

Obviously, the intention of any entrepreneur is to get a reward at the end of his/her endeavor. Through growth hacking, you will carry out A/B testing (testing of two product variants, e.g. product A and Product B). Revenue metrics of both products will help you understand which product is preferable to customers. This will help you focus on that product and enhance it through further testing.

For more information on Revenue, read section on "Monetization techniques"

Referral – Do users tell others?

Referral is the greatest endorsement an entrepreneur can ever receive. Referrals come from satisfied customers who recommend others to your product. Metrics on referrals are important in determining customer loyalty. The entire concept of growth hacking, that is, virality, wholly depends on referral.

For more information on Referral, read "Customer retention".

How to prepare growth hacking project

Growth hacking is a recursive process. Thus, it involves the following process in which the first eventually becomes the last as the cycle completes and begins;

1. Set strategic goals

2. Gather and analyze data

3. Generate hypothesis

4. Prioritize experiments

5. Design and implement tests

6. Analyze results

7. Systemize

How to develop a growth hack product

The following are the crucial steps to creating a growth hack product;

1. Creating the product that markets itself

2. Engage the user to find the growth hack

3. Hacking your way to virality

4. Retention

1. Create a product that markets itself

The only product that markets itself is that product that solves a problem. Thus, it is a solution in itself. To create a product that is a solution, you need a two-step process:

- Minimum Viable Product (MVP) – This is the basic solution. This is like a blueprint. This is what you achieve through research on various data sets.

- Product Market Fit (PMF) – This is the ultimate solution derived from the blueprint but hacked for growth through user engagement, participation and A/B testing.

2. Engage the user to find your growth hack

User engagement and participation is vital for a growth hack. Growth hacking employs various technologies to measure and determine user experience. These technologies include A/B testing, analyzing acquisition metrics, pondering on activation metrics and using feedback tools such as social media, survey questionnaires, forums, chats and others to gain feedback.

At the end of it, this engagement and feedback is solely for purposes of deriving Product Market Fit (PMF).

3. Hack your way to virality

Virality is about mass acquisition through referrals. A PMF solution brings such a great combination of 'halo' and 'aha' effects which inspires and compels users to share it out with others.

First, without a PMF solution, virality cannot be possible. Yes, the quality must be guaranteed. Once the quality is guaranteed, the next thing is to engineer the spread and velocity with which this PMF flows. It is this rate of spread and velocity that is viral.

The following are the various hacks to boost virality;

- Commissions, rebates, discounts on referrals

- Freebies on subscription

4. Retain customers through discovery, education and engagement

Customers are students who are eager to learn about your proposed solution. Like any student, there is nothing as inspiring as graduating with a distinction. If you have ever graduated, then, you know how you feel on your graduation day and how that feeling spreads to your loved ones.

Like a teacher, it is the intent of a growth hacker to produce this great experience. Thus, the growth hacker must keep on exploring new discoveries, educating his customers on these new discoveries and engaging customers on how to utilize and benefit from these new discoveries.

Yes, there are many universities out there, but, the Ivy League retains the crème de la crème to nothing more than discovery, education and engagement. You too can achieve this. As we have seen, a growth hackers' foremost objective is building communities around his products, just as a great university focuses on building communities around its education.

Strategy

Your strategy should be laid out by answering the following key questions;

1. How do I soar up the levels of acquisition? e.g. getting more signups

2. What should I do to activate as many acquisitions (customers, clients, users, etc) as possible within the first target period (e.g. 30 days)?

3. What are the key levers of engagement and how can I pull them?

Answering these key questions will enable you to identify products that have a profound impact on your key metrics (e.g. acquisitions). This way, you can choose to:

1. Optimize those channels that will result in more acquisitions

2. Build new channels that can boost acquisitions, either as an addition to the existing channels or as a replacement of those channels that are not capable of being optimized.

Growth Hacking Strategy

1. Educate Your Audience

Education is an essential part of any PR strategy. Education means creating engaging content that helps prospects understand your industry.

2. Leverage Social Media Analytics to Target the Right People

Social media analytics can offer you credible insights that can help you find the right people create the right message and make a timely delivery. For example, Event Targeting, an analytical feature offered by Twitter can enable you to find people based on upcoming industry events that they attend. This helps you to define demographics, interests and engagement strategies to employ on your target audience.

3. Use Free (or Low-Cost) Tools Whenever Possible

As a startup, you want to keep your budget low while aiming high. Thus, it is certainly prudent to utilize free or low-cost tools available to you.

The following are great tools that you can use;

- **Google Analytics** – This is a free analytics tool offered to you by Google.

- **Help Reporter Out (HARO**) - that can easily boost your PR endeavors. It connects bloggers, PR professionals and Journalists.

- **BuzzSumo** – This tool helps you keep updated on latest market trends and provides information on key influencers. The influencer information can help you be abreast with competition as it informs you of the key competitors in your industry.

- **<u>24-7 press release</u>** – This is a press release service. You can write your press release and grant it for wide distribution at an affordable plan. This is one of the ways to boost your visibility.

- **<u>MuckRack</u>** – This is great for PR professionals. It not only helps you monitor conversations about your company but also provides you with an alert about new PR opportunities that you can engage in.

4. Repurpose Your Content

It is time consuming and costly to write new content. Content expires over time, unless it is evergreen. Whichever the case, boost relevance and reach, it is necessary to regenerate, renew, repackage and reinvigorate it through repurposing.

You can repurpose old content by;

- Using infographics

- Repackaging the message

- Creating an eBook from a series of blogs

5. Constantly Test and Improve Your Strategy

Use A/B testing to keep experimentation on what kind of content attracts your audience.

6. Become Part of Virtual Communities in Your Industry

Participate in virtual communities relevant to your industry. Quora and Warrior forums are great places. Stack Overflow is a great place if you are a programmer.

7. Leave a Digital Trail

If you are engaging on a project that will take long to accomplish, it is great to keep your audience updated. Share photos and information on the latest updates. This helps to enhance following. Thus, you are more likely to convert the audience that has been following you throughout the process.

Tips to effect growth hacking strategy

1. Use ad extensions to get targeted clicks

2. Inject your funnel with content upgrade offers such as free report or eBook

3. Strategically use giveaways to inspire buzz and traffic – Giveaways help to draw attention towards your brand,

generate traffic and boost your potential of getting prospective subscribers whom you can convert.

The following are some of the giveaways you can provide:

- Sample products

- BoGo (Buy One, Get One) offers

- Trial VIP access to tiered pricing discounts

- Free introductory products

- Reward-based incentives

Giveaways can also help you gain user-generated content such as product endorsements, positive reviews, etc, which helps to boost your trust in the eyes of potential customers.

4. Incite urgency by creating FOMO hysteria - Fear of Missing Out (FOMO) is one of the effective marketing tactics that have been used over time to initiate conversion by instigating a sense of urgency in the customer's psychology. Take advantage of FOMO by creating limited one-time promotions, contests, and content offers.

5. Build LTV through exemplary after-sale customer service – After closing a sale, follow-up on your customers to keep them updated and engaged. Custom email campaigns, newsletters and magazines are a great way to keep customers engaged, build loyalty improve retention rate and boost lifetime value (LTV) of your customers.

6. Find and engage your influencers – Every industry has its own influencers. Influencers are trusted in the eyes of consumers. They are their independent and reliable source of advice, opinions and information regarding latest trends. Engaging influencers into your marketing campaign can have a great impact. Studies have found out that social media influencers can help to generate two times more sales than paid social adverts. Create an impression of your ideal influencer, search out and reach out for one who best-fits your impression to make a personal connection and mutually develop the best value exchange.

7. Create an "on-ramp" for new customers. An on-ramp is simply a new entry access point. New users struggle to find different ways to utilize a given product. Ecommerce On-ramp support could include;

   • Use of drip campaigns strategically designed to 'drip' consumable pieces of information one at a time, in a timed interval.

- Accentuating important features and providing feature-specific instructions.

- Providing animated tour guides for various product usage scenarios.

Animations, videos, images, voice-overs, etc are great tools that you can use to implement the 'on-ramps'

8. Streamline the checkout process – Studies have shown that about 68% of shopping carts are abandoned which costs an estimated $4.9 trillion in sales globally. Thus, streamlining your checkout process can greatly help you to avoid these costs.

The following are the common friction points that result into abandonment;

- Complicated site and checkout navigation

- Site-security concerns

- Lack of information (shipping details, customer support details, etc.)

- Pricing issues (un-anticipated bundled products consuming extra cost)

- Lengthy forms

- Being forced to create an account

- Shipping costs

9. Use psychology in your pricing – It is hard to anticipate a consumer's purchasing power or budgetary provision. Thus, it is important to provide multiple purchase options such as multiple subscriptions option, so that you can cater for more diverse consumers.

10. Trigger offline social share – Take advantage of the peak excitement moment at delivery by making a surprise offer such as promotional code, discount on subsequent purchase, reward on referral, custom hash-tag of your brand on social media, etc.

11. Create and promote your referral program – Studies have shown that 83% of satisfied consumers are willing to refer friends and loved ones to a brand but only 29% do it. To increase the referral potential, do ask them to do so. Also offer some referral incentives. Find the most appropriate referral, whether monetary or non-monetary or a combination to boost the referral rate.

12. Increase trust through product reviews on social media.

13. Develop smart retargeting strategies – Just about 2% of customers get activated on their visit. This may be due to being on the wrong device at the appropriate moment or missing the right device at the appropriate moment. Thus, to ensure that your promotion effort is available to them, you must retarget your customers on multiple devices. You must use tools that keep track of customer activity online so that the same advert presented on one device will still be strategically available on the other device that the customer uses.

14. Use segment-targeted drip email campaigns – drip email campaigns enhance customer loyalty. Use email tools such as Mail Chimp to schedule and automate your emails.

BUILDING A TEAM OF GROWTH

Building a team of growth hackers is the most fundamental step in growth hacking. The following are important considerations to make as you build this team;

1. Characteristic traits of a growth hacker

2. Key competencies of a growth hacker

3. The size of the team that you want to build

4. The growth team model

What are the characteristic traits of a growth hacker?

The following are characteristics that you should look for in a growth hacker

- Data-driven thinker

- Rapid learner

- Comprehensive understanding of growth process

- Product-savvy

- Hustle mindset

- Link marketing with product development

- Technical acumen – Coding, data visualization, growth analytics, web scrapping, financial acumen,

- Creative problem solver

- Commitment towards achieving sustainable, scalable growth.

- In-depth understanding and appreciation how people work, think, and feel.

- Focused on growth – They are always finding ways to growth their brands and themselves

- Passionate about metrics– They pay attention to metrics

- Action-driven – They actualize their thoughts and words

- Effective time manager– They prioritize based on what counts to growth

- Replicates success – Find ways to instigate replication of their successful endeavors

- Vision-minded– Visualize where they ought to be and works towards achieving the vision

- Open-minded and receptive to new ideas – Seeks new ideas and get inspired about them.

What are the key competencies to look for in a growth hacker?

- Creative problem solver

- Big thinking

- Scientific approach

- Marketing nous

- Technical know-how

- Focus-oriented (focus management)

- Obsession for growth

- Knowledge in consumer psychology

What size of a team do you need?

There are three basic startup levels depending on your enterprise resource capability;

1. Less than 10

2. Between 10 and 15

3. More than 15

Startup team for a small enterprise

1. Head of Growth

   Key competencies:

   - Strong personality traits

   - Highly creative

   - Strong analytical flair

   - Great soft skills

   - Process-driven

2. Developer

   Key competencies:

   - Highly creative

   - Growth focused

   - Fast executor

   - Prioritizes quick building over fixing

   - Great flair for data manipulation, tracking and analytics

- Astronomical iteration

3. User Interface /User Experience

   Key competencies:

   - Emotionally intelligent

   - Impressive front-end coding skills

   - Prioritizes quick building over fixing

   - Fast executor

   - Enjoys testing

4. Data analyst

   Key competencies:

   Good analytic flair with both small and large data sets

   Impressive back-end knowledge

   Extremely keen on details

   Great data insights

Choosing a growth team model

There are two growth team models:

- Independent model

- Functional model

Independent model

This is a model where an organization is structured based on the various independent growth levers or unique features within a particular growth lever.

Example of lever-based model:

The following managers would be under a **VP Growth**;

- Product Manager – Acquisition

- Product Manager – Activation

- Product Manager – Retention

- Product Manager – Revenue

- Product Manager – Referrals

Example of feature-based model:

The following managers would be under VP Growth;

- Product Manager – Signups

- Product Manager – On-boarding

- Product Manager – Notifications

Apart from the VP Growth, there would be VP Product, VP Engineering, and VP Marketing. All of them are under the CEO.

Adopters of this model include Facebook and Uber.

Functional model

This is a model where the organization is structured according to functions. These functions include:

- Activities

- Actions

- Processes

- Operations

Example of function-based model:

The following managers would be under **VP Product**;

- Product Manager – Signups

- Product Manager – On-boarding

- Product Manager – Notifications

Apart from the VP Product, there would be VP Engineering, VP Marketing. All of them are under the CEO.

Adopters of this model include Twitter, Pinterest, LinkedIn, BitTorrent and Dropbox.

A Message from the Author

Hey, are you enjoying the book? I'd love to hear your thoughts!

Many readers do not know how hard reviews are to come by, and how much they help an author.

I would be incredibly thankful if you could take just 60 seconds to write a brief review on Amazon, even if it's just a few sentences!

Please head to the product page, and leave a review as shown below.

Customer Reviews

⭐⭐⭐⭐⭐ 2

5.0 out of 5 stars ▾

5 star		100%
4 star		0%
3 star		0%
2 star		0%

Share your thoughts with other customer

Write a customer review

Thank you for taking the time to share your thoughts!

IDENTIFYING YOUR GROWTH LEVERS

A growth lever is any component that represents a strategic opportunity for a brand to accelerate its growth.

It is important to understand the growth levers of your brand. These are the gears which you can manipulate to accelerate your brand to greater growth levels. If you don't know them, then, it would be impossible to focus. Also, without knowing them, it is impossible to have predictable, scalable and recursive achievements.

In growth hacking, the following are five main levers; Acquisition, Activation, Retention, Revenue and Referrals. These are already known. However, their key drivers are not identical from one firm to the next. Yet, how to apply them will also vary from one firm to another. Just like vehicles on the road, each driver is unique, even though they could have the basic driving license. Also, each driver drives a different kind of vehicle e.g. saloon car, minibus, heavy truck, etc.

To be able to identify your brand's growth driver, you need to have a deeper reflection and understanding of your customer as the key stakeholder. In this regard, you need to take a three-step process;

1. Examine your brand's strategic objective – What is your brand trying to achieve strategically? Critically analyze your brand plans and understand the thinking behind the strategic objectives. The strategic objectives are determined by strategic goals.

2. Identify the key customers you are trying to win and methods that you are using to achieve that.

3. Get your metrics right – Use pirate metrics to identify performance of your growth levers.

What are the levers are used to propel the success of a growth hack?

The following are the levers and their respective drivers which are used to propel the success of a growth hack:

Acquisition – How do users find you?

Key driver: Customer attraction

Tactics: SEO, SEM, PR, Social Media, Content Marketing, Business Development, Referrals, Free trials, Newsletter, Guest Posts, Outreach, Q & A

For in-depth information on acquisition read the section on "Attracting customers"

Activation – Do users have a great first experience?

Key drivers:

- First impressions

- Engagement and education

- Follow Up

Tactics: Social Media, Content Marketing, Newsletter, Lead nurturing, On-boarding, screen casts, blank states

For more information on activation, read section on "First impressions", "Engage and Educate" and "Follow Up"

Retention – Do users come back?

Key driver: Customer retention

For incisive details on customer retention, read section on "Customer retention",

Revenue – How do you make money?

Key driver: Monetization techniques

For a greater perspective on Revenue, read section on "Monetization techniques"

Referral – Do users tell others?

Key driver: Customer retention

For more information on Referral, read "Customer retention".

ATTRACTING CUSTOMERS

Attracting customers is a key driver to customer acquisition. There are several ways to acquire customers. However, all of them fall into two main categories;

- Inbound acquisition

- Outbound acquisition

Inbound acquisition

Inbound acquisition refers to those 'in-house' ways of acquiring customers. These include:

- Landing pages

- SEO

- Social channels

- Content creation

- Running a blog

We shall have a deeper perspective on each of these inbound acquisition methods in the section titled "Engage and Educate", later in this book.

Outbound acquisition

Outbound acquisition refers to those external ways of acquiring customers. They include:

- Billboards

- Radio and TV adverts

- Person-to-person sales promotion

- Paid media – e.g. Pay Per Click

- Sponsorships – e.g. Sponsoring athletes (Puma, Adidas, etc, sponsoring programs, etc)

- Attending Meet-ups (trade fairs, exhibitions, professional talk shows, etc)

- Email marketing

Radio and TV adverts, billboards and sponsorships are rarely used as they are not only expensive for startups but also not as determinable as internet-based methods.

Three stages of customer acquisition

The following are important stages for customer acquisition in a growth hack. They are applicable where customers are granted trial/sample products with the hope of them transitioning to the activation stage.

1. Attraction

2. Convert

3. Close

Attraction

This involves any campaign or activity aimed at attracting customers to a product/service center. This center could be your website, store, etc.

Convert

This involves consistently reviewing the customer acquisition journey to optimize conversion

Close

This involves optimizing user experiences such that the user decides to take up what is on offer

The growth matrix: Tracking and reporting growth

The three key matrices you need to be concerned about are;

1. Total unique traffic to product/service center (attract) – e.g. your web page – click through rate

2. How many of those unique visitors get to try your product/service (conversion) – e.g. conversion rate

3. How many take up your product (close)

Activity vs. goal: Make the difference

Activities are not goals. Activities not aligned with goals are dummy activities.

For example:

Activity 1: Writing weekly sales report

Goal: boost sales by 15%

Activity 2: Conclusively handling customer complaints and challenges

Goal: Reduce customer turnover by 20%

Activity 3: Meeting biweekly to discuss new product development

Goal: Launch 3 new products by end of this half-year

Activity 4: Take part in quality control training program

Goal: Reduce wastage by 25%

Consequences of failure to set goals

- Rewarding activities not geared towards organizational goals

- Lack of team responsibility towards attainment of set goals

- Waste of time and resources engaging in dummy activities (activities that add no value to the organizations wealth)

Setting SMARTEST GOALS

A goal enables you to:

1. Have a direction

2. Be focused

3. Plan on what you can do to achieve your ultimate end

4. Be disciplined

5. Can measure your success

A SMARTEST goal must be:

- **Specific** – It should have a focus in mind e.g. growth

- **Measurable** – It should have clear metrics to measure it

- **Achievable** – It must be such that you can achieve it.

- **Realistic** – It must meet both your willpower and ability

- **Timely** – It must have an executable timeframe

- **Empowering** – It should be able to inspire, motivate and ignite action

- **Sensual** – It should be able to arouse greater imaginative experience

- **Transformational** – It should be able to radically change the status of things.

Customer Acquisition tactics

1. Encouraging users to spread the word through carefully crafted referral program

2. Employ strategic means of finding customers online

3. Use content marketing

4. Use email marketing and nurturing

5. Use SEO

6. Use Paid acquisition using targeting & remarketing –e.g. PPC

7. Use A/B testing, analytics and data to drive decision-making

8. Optimize every successful endeavor

9. Use Agile and lean development to boost user experience

FIRST IMPRESSIONS

In psychology, it is known that first impression lasts forver. This also applies to consumer psychology. Thus, whether you will move your potential lead from the acquisition to the activation stage depends on your first impression. It is very critical. You cannot afford to ignore it.

Why are first impressions such important?

First impression is an important step in building lasting relationships. First impression is just as important in your formal relationships as it is in informal relationships. Stakeholder relationships need a great first impression. These stakeholder relationships include customer relationships, investor relationships, vendor relationships, shareholder relationships, community relationships, government agency relationships, among such other formal relationships. At one stage in your growth process, you will need these relationships.

Personal vs. Enterprise impressions

Personal impressions are those impressions expressed by human beings. Enterprise (organizational) impressions are those formed by corporate enterprises.

Enterprise impressions gain their existence due to personal impressions. Thus, they depict wholesome collective impressions of individuals within an organization. Yet, by system principle, a whole is not equal to the sum of independent parts. This is because, the organization will acquire new and unique attributes of its own that are not necessarily representative of the collection of attributes of individuals who comprise it.

Thus, as we look at enterprise impressions, we must not ignore these unique enterprise attributes that are independent of the individuals that comprise it.

What are the core elements of first personal impressions?

There are two core elements of first impression:

- Mental predisposition (attitude)

- Physical predisposition (posture)

- Emotional predisposition (temperament)

How do you make a great first impression through physical predisposition?

The first impression revolves around these three core domains;

- Body

- Dress

- Address

Body

Your body is the physical you. This physical you can be visual (in case of face to face encounter) or non-visual (in case of non-facial encounter such as voice or text conversations). However, even with no face-to-face encounter, there are some elements of your body that are transmitted to the recipient. For example, your tone - in case of voice conversation and your copywriting prowess - in terms of text conversation.

We shall see the body language under address. But, as now, let's focus on your body's appearance as a first impression (even though dressed).

The physical elements of your body that can make a lasting impression include;

- Scent

- Skin form

- Sweat

How to make a great first impressing through proper body form:

1. Ensure good hygiene.

- Bathe before making any business engagement and stay clean.

- Wash your mouth often - At least 3 times including before going to bed, immediately upon waking up and after every meal. When you are not taking meals (more so, when fasting) brush your teeth at least three times during the day (excluding wake-up time and bed time). It is more common to have bad breath when you are hungry.

2. Make sure you ooze out a great scent – have a neutral scent. Take care of those parts of the body.

Dress

Well, most of your body is dressed, especially when it comes to formal engagements. Thus, how you dress matters a lot as a first impression.

Wear more formal than your intended audience.

Address

How you address those that you encounter at first will leave a lasting impression. Addressing has everything to do with communication. In this communication, there are two elements:

- Verbal

- Non-verbal

Verbal communication refers to that form of communication where you express yourself either orally or in writing. For a great impression during verbal communication;

- Have the right tone

- Face your audience directly

- Make them feel at ease

- Be entertaining

Non-verbal communication refers to that form of communication where you don't express yourself in a verbal way. This is mainly through body language which includes signs, symbols, posture and such other forms of body language.

The key elements of your non-verbal communication that must stand out are;

- Welcoming – A radiant smile, a warm handshake

- Professional

- Astute

- Confident

- Brave

- Courteous

- Attentive

How to make a great first online enterprise impression

1. Have a fast-loading landing page

2. Have a great looking website

3. Have a memorable logo

4. Have organized menus each leading to the core areas of customer interest

5. Enhance user experience through image optimization, easy navigation, good color schemes

6. Provide great presentation e.g. through animation, slides, etc.

7. Organize your product store

8. Have a featured product page with prompting links to appropriate demos and trials

9. Have easy to scan, clear and concise content.

10. Provide a welcoming chat feature

ENGAGE AND EDUCATE

Engagement refers to creating an experience designed to connect a solution to the user's problems with enough frequency to form a habit.

Education and engagement is geared towards using value content to promote understanding and user interaction.

The following are key steps by which you build up your list, and keep them educated and engaged in the process:

- Create a social-media-friendly piece of content – The content should be informative, entertaining, easily digestible and irresistible to forego. Use of videos, animations and bullet points are some of the ways to achieve this

- Use social media advertising to promote your piece of content – Depending on your target audience, you can use Twitter Advertising, Facebook Advertising, Youtube Advertising, Taboola or Outbrain to promote your piece of content.

- Provide plenty of avenues by which they can opt-in to the source – The purpose of advertising is to pull potential audience to a source (target). Providing relevant links to the target in the adverts is a must.

- Create a remarketing tag – Tagging is important when it comes to social media advertising.

- Use remarketing tags to remarket offers to the audience – Offer solutions to the audience, not products. This easily makes them find the value in your offer. It is only after finding a solution to their problem that they can get inspired to access your product.

Blogging hacks

Why blogs are a great tool for marketing strategy:

From studies, it has been established that:

1. Enterprises with blogs generate 97% more inbound links.

2. Effective onsite company blogs results into 55% more visitors.

3. 70% of customers prefer being educated via blog articles rather than advertisements.

Onsite blog hacks

To have an effective onsite company blog;

1. Effectively utilize SEO – Do thorough keyword research to have effective keywords that you can formulate into your content

2. Create great content – The content should be unique, informative and engaging.

3. Build trust and authority – Persistently and consistently provide valuable content to the users so as to provide clear-cut solutions. Now, your audience trusts your content. This enables you to become an authority in your niche.

4. Focus on organic traffic – Blending effective SEO and great helpful content with generate organic traffic. Organic traffic is that which comes without you endeavoring to advertise. Organic traffic is less costly and long-term.

5. Create a lasting brand impression – Strategically choreograph content in such a manner that your subject matter can be easily visualized and memorized. Using creative tools such as animation, infographics, videos, etc, can help in visualization and easy memorization. In

addition, don't forget to use your brand logo and product labels to enhance brand recognition.

6. Create great relationships – Business is about relationships. Every growth hacker endeavors to build communities around his/her solution. Thus, it is important to create content in an engaging conversational manner so that the audience feels you are talking to them. You can pose questions and even provide some of the most likely answers from them. Through content, you can build your brand voice and win loyalty.

7. Inform your customers – Informing customers is a great way to show them that you care about their need to know. Let know of your future launches, new product features that you are considering, etc. This way, they keep on anticipating and getting prepared. They will be readier to purchase the new product once launched. Also, as a growth hacker, this is a way you can test their feelings and perspectives and thus be able to modify your product or incorporate more features for maximum impact.

8. Boost engagement – Let your blog not just be of static content. Have chat features, forums, and comment section so that you can engage your audience. If it is not possible to make a 24/7 arrangement to be available (maybe because you don't have other people to help or scenarios

require you), let your audience know your availability schedule well in advance.

Offsite blog hacks

1. Use Visual Content – Visuals sink faster and deeper than text. Use visuals to enhance memorization of your text. Photos, symbols, charts, tables, infographics are great way to enhance visualization.

2. Keep It Short – Have short headlines with a brief body.

3. Keep It Simple – Avoid complicating things. Be concise.

4. Make Your Content Easy to Digest – Content structure matters. Use short sentences and short paragraphs. Have memorable keywords. Use simple terms. Use examples that are easy to relate and unforgettable.

5. Know Your Audience – Do extensive research to know who your target audience is and what kind of information they are looking for. Furthermore, get to know what excites them and drive them.

6. Arrange and Design – Make your blog post well organized with elements properly arranged and seamlessly flowing.

Make a perfect combination of image, content, color scheme and navigation.

7. Connect the Dots – Know your audience, anticipate what they need to know. Connect the dots between their knowledge and what they need to know.

8. Know What Direction You're Going In – Make sure your next steps lead to your final goal

9. Be Lucid – Maintain clarity of purpose throughout your engagement. Be focused to your goal.

10. Keep Track of What Works – Employ metrics to know exactly what pulls and moves your audience.

11. Grab Their Attention – Use ways and means to grab attention. Learn how Clickhole and Buzzfeed have done it.

12. Persevere and End Strong – Think about the future. Leave a lasting impression. Build a legacy.

Social Media Growth hacks

Social media enhances engagement, increases visibility and builds following

To achieve success:

1. Optimize your profile

2. Research your market

3. Ensure consistency

4. Be prepared for long-term engagement

5. Build lasting relationships

Optimize your profile

To optimize your profile, include important information such as

- About – Provide all relevant information about you. This will enable others to have a clear impression of who you are, what you do, and what they expect from you.

- Contact – Provide up to date contact details including your website url, email address, telephone address, WhatsApp address, physical address (if applicable), among others.

- Image – Provide a good business logo and brand/product image.

Research your market

You must know whom you need to interact with to create content that matches your target goals and objectives.

Ensure consistency

Be consistent about your subject matter across various social media networks. This helps to boost brand identity and recognition.

Be prepared for long-term engagement

To create a productive mass following on social media is not a short-term endeavor. You must know it is a long-term endeavor

Build relationships, not sales

Don't use your social media for a sales pitch. Rather, use your social media to build relationships with your potential customers. This way, they won't see you as a salesperson nor them as vulnerable customers; but you as a solution provider and them as partners.

Tips for effective social media engagement:

- Select the most appropriate social media channel for your brand

- Be patient and consistent

- Listen to and engage your audience while focusing on their personal interests

- Interact with them beyond just communicating

- Reach out and engage with influencers

- Be ready to adjust and adapt to changing social media dynamics

- Embrace the weird – be different, be creative, and this will propel curiosity, interest and love.

- Let them see behind the curtain – it's still about who you are, where you've been and what you have to offer

- Differentiate between your suspects, prospects, leads and opportunities, and learn how to serve each respectively.

- Take advantage of social media metrics for your content strategy.

FOLLOW UP

Follow up is the act and process of exploring more interactions with potential leads with the sole purpose of closing a sale.

Why do it?

The intent of follow up is to convert a potential lead into a customer and thus close a sale.

Follow up system

A follow up system varies depending on the sales system that you use. The traditional sales system is different from the growth hacking system.

Qualities of a good follow up system;

- Systematic processing

- Minimal effort (labor efficient)

- Predictable and consistent outcome

Follow up strategies:

- Timing – You should make your follow-ups timely. Having a pre-arranged schedule based on past experience and metrics analysis will help you to predict the most appropriate timing. However, this should be customized to suit a customer's particular circumstances.

- Regularity – Let follow-ups be regular. A pre-arranged schedule is ideal. In case of email, using auto-emailing tools is great. This allows you to create follow-up messages early in advanced for release at regular interval, each based on a previous feedback. However, the messages must be custom and relevant to the feedback flow.

- Relevance – Follow-ups, though timely and regular, must not sacrifice relevance. They should be particular to the subject matter at hand.

Follow up secrets/tips

1. Cherry-picking

2. Timing

3. Integrate (sales and marketing) various techniques

4. Enliven your database

5. Education, repetition and variety

- Educate – Provide valuable information

- Repetition – Keep repeating core points in different ways

- Mix various tools of follow up – e.g. chatting, email, telephone contact, webinars, etc

Follow-up tactics

- Act on leads, don't sit on them

- Understand what people want and when

- Focus on the hottest leads

- Maximize on CRM (Customer Relationship Management)

- Use marketing automation

- Think about your channel

- Be prepared

- Learn from your website

- Know your numbers (metrics)

To make follow up successful:

1. Intuitively ask for guidance from the customers on the best way to follow up with them while adding value without being annoying.

2. Ask customers what their preferred form of communication is and if they will respond.

3. Make sure you always end conversation with a clear information on the next step.

4. Summarize your conversation and get written confirmation.

5. Have specific reasons to contact your prospect.

Post-sales follow up

- Say thank you – As a sign of appreciation

- Do a check-in – To reaffirm to your customer that he/she made the right choice

- Keep lines of communication open – To offer high value content such as guides, webinars

- Think of more sales opportunities – Such as complementary products

- Tactically ask for referrals

Benefits of post sale follow up

- Boost sales

- Increase customer retention

- Generate customer testimonials and referrals

- Improve your performance

- Increase your innovative prowess – Understanding your customer's needs and challenges provides you with in-depth intelligence that helps you to create new and unique products and services.

- Differentiation – Through your follow up you differentiate yourself from the crowd of other sellers.

How to avoid redundant calls

There are times you need to make a follow up call as part of your schedule. Yet, you seem to be struggling with what the call ought to be about. Instead of saying "I was just getting in touch", find creative ways to fill up. The following are three better options:

1. Re-emphasize the business value

2. Share ideas and insights

3. Continue to educate

MONETIZATION TECHNIQUES

Monetization falls is a term growth hacking of revenue. Monetization techniques are determined by the particular monetization model that you choose to employ.

Monetization models

There are many monetization models for growth hacking. Whichever should be your choice depends on your nature of enterprise. The following are the main models of monetization;

- Commerce

- Subscriptions (membership)

- Transaction processing

- Data

- Peer-to-Peer

- Licensing

- Mobile

- Gaming

- Advertisement

Commerce:

1. Digital goods – Downloadable products such as music, videos, tutorials, podcasts, iTunes, etc.

2. Commission per order - Seamless, GrubHub, etc

3. Vertically Integrated Commerce - Warby Parker

4. Marketplace - Amazon Marketplace, Etsy, etc

5. Virtual goods - Zynga

6. Crowdsourced Marketplace - Threadless

7. Auction - eBay

8. Aggregator - Lastminute.com

9. Pay what you want - Radiohead

10. Idle Capacity Market - Uber, AirBnB

11. Training - Coursera

12. Retailing - Zappos

13. Barter for services - SwapRight

14. Flash Sales - Vente Privee, Gilt Groupe

15. Group buying - Groupon

16. Commission - SharesPost

17. Reverse Auction - Priceline

Subscriptions (membership)

1. Sampling – Birchbox

2. PAAS (Platform as a Service) - AWS

3. SAAS (Software as a Service) - Salesforce

4. Voice and video-conferencing - Uberconference

5. Donations - Wikipedia

6. Support and Maintenance - Red Hat, 10gen

7. Content as a Service - Netflix, Spotify

8. Freemium SAAS - Dropbox

9. Service as a Service - Shopify

10. Paywall - New York Times

11. Membership Services - Amazon Prime

Transaction processing

1. Fulfillment - Amazon

2. Bank Transfer - Dwolla

3. Merchant Acquiring - Stripe, PayPal, Square

4. Payment Gateways: Mobile - Braintree

5. Bank Card Issuance - Simple

6. Telephony - Skype

7. Acquiring Processing - Paymentech

8. Bank Depository Offering - Movenbank, Simple

9. Platform Monetization - Facebook Credits

10. Intermediary - CardSpring, IP Commerce

11. Messaging - IM, P2PSMS, Group Messaging

Data

1. Market research - GLG

2. Search Data - Chango

3. User data - BlueKai

4. Benchmarking services - Comscore

5. User intelligence - Yougov

6. Real-time Consumer Intent Data - Yieldbot

7. Business data - Duedil

Peer-to-peer

1. P2P Mobile resource sharing - Mobile Wi-Fi/Tethering

2. P2P insurance/home/car

3. P2P Lending - Lending Club

4. P2P service - TaskRabbit, Mechanical Turk

5. P2P buying - Etsy

6. P2P computing - SETI@home, CrasPlan storage

7. P2P Gambling - BetFair

Licensing

1. Indirect Licensing - Apple Volume Purchasing

2. Site License (Per) -   Private cloud on internal infrastructure

3. Seat License (Per) - Sencha

4. Brand Licensing - Sesame Street

5. Application instance (Per) - Adobe Photoshop

6. Patent Licensing - Qualcomm

7. Device/Server License (Per) - QlikView

Mobile

1. Advertising - Flurry, AdMob

2. App Downloads (Paid)- WhatsApp

3. Transactions - Hailo

4. App subscriptions (In-app) - NY Times app

5. Digital-to-physical - Postagram, Red Stamp

6. App purchases (In-app) - Zynga Poker

Gaming

1. Downloadable Content (DLC) - Call of Duty

2. Freemium - Zynga

3. Premium - xBox games

4. Ad Supported - addictinggames.co

5. Subscription- World of Warcraft

Advertisement

1. Real-time Intent Ad Delivery

2. Paid content links - Outbrain

3. Video Ads - Hulu

4. Sponsorships / Site Takeovers - Pandora

5. Display Ads - Yahoo!

6. Classifieds - Craiglist

7. Promoted Content - Tumblr, Twitter

8. Lead Generation - ZocDoc, MoneySuperMarket

9. Email Ads - MSN, Yahoo

10. Location-based offers - Foursquare

11. Audio Ads - Pandora

12. Audio Ads - Pandora

13. Featured listings - Super Pages, Yelp

14. Search Ads - Google

15. Ad Retargeting - Criteo

16. Affiliate Fees - Amazon Affiliate Program

17. Recruitment Ads - LinkedIn

GROWTH HACKING TECHNOLOGGIES

Growth hacking technologies refer to a special combination of tools and techniques that makes it easy to hack into growth.

The following are the main categories of growth hacking technologies;

- STPO (marketing) technologies

- Management technologies

- Analytical technologies

- Entrepreneurial technologies

- Content technologies

- Social engagement technologies

STPO (marketing) technologies

- Segmentation – Segment your customers into various categories

- Targeting – This is filtering your audience as per certain criteria (e.g. demographics, segment, etc) and then customize your focus on them.

- Positioning – This refers to carefully putting your brand into strategically placed position compared to other competing brands.

- Optimization – This refers to perpetually devising, testing, refining your existing and new products.

Management technologies

- Project Management

Analytical technologies

- Statistics

- A/B Testing

- Digital analytics

Coding technologies

- Web and Mobile Programming

- Database SQL

Entrepreneurial technologies

- Ecommerce – Web commerce

- Mcommerce – Mobile commerce

Content management technologies

- Copywriting

- Blogging

- SEO

- Linkbuilding

Social engagement technologies

- Facebook blogging

- Twitter blogging

- Instagram

Growth Hacking Tools

There is a huge array of great growth hacking tools that you can use to boost your growth hacking endeavor. These tools fall into the following main categories

1. Traffic acquisition

2. Lead and customer acquisition

3. Market research and user feedback

4. Email marketing

5. Inbound marketing and marketing automation

6. Analytics

7. Content boost/exposure

8. SEO

9. A/B Testing

10. Public Relations

11. Gmail plugins (General)

12. Others

Traffic Acquisition

1. Colibri.io

2. Pay with A Tweet

3. Click to Tweet

4. Nimble

5. MixRank

6. Twilighter

Lead & Customer Acquisition

1. Hello Bar

2. Bounce Exchange

3. SessionCam

4. KISSmetrics

5. CrazyEgg

6. Totango

7. Unbounce

8. Optimizely

9. Visual Website Optimizer

10. Clicktale

11. Coastics

12. Zapier

13. Gumroad

Market Research & User Feedback

1. Qualaroo

2. Consumer Baromoter

3. Typeform

4. Polldaddy

5. Olark

Email Marketing

1. ListBuilder

2. Vero

3. MailChimp

4. AWeber

5. SendGrid

6. sendwithus

7. Customer.io

8. Klaviyo

Inbound Marketing & Marketing Automation

1. Infusion Soft

2. HubSpot

3. Marketo

Analytics

1. Clkim

2. Bounce Exchange / BounceX

3. SessionCam

4. KISSmetrics

5. MixPanel

6. Clicktale

7. Crazy Egg

8. Qualaroo

Content Boosts / Exposure

1. BuzzSumo

2. Canva

3. Grammarly

4. Sniply

5. Gumroad

6. Click to Tweet

7. FameBit

SEO

1. Colibri

2. SemRush

3. Mobile Action

A/B Testing

1. Optimizely

2. Visual Website Optimizer

Social Media

1. Buffer

2. Dux Soup

3. LinkedIn Helper

4. HypeGrowth

5. InstaRanker

PR (Public Relations)

1. JustReachOut

2. PRServe

Gmail Plugins

1. Yet Another Mail Merge (YAMM)

2. Boomerang

3. Streak

4. Rapportive

Others

1. Queue (Referral Marketing / Viral Growth)

2. InviteReferrals (Referral Marketing / Viral Growth)

3. Customer.io (Personalization)

4. Trello (Management / Organization)

5. Slack (Collaboration / Company Chat)

6. UpWork (Freelance Hiring)

7. Apifier (Web Scraping)

8. Totango (Prospection/Conversions)

9. Consumer Barometer (Strategize)

10. LastPass (Password Protection)

CUSTOMER RETENTION

Customer retention refers to strategically enabling customers to perpetually buy your products and services.

Why is retention so important?

Studies have shown that:

- Getting a new customer 25 times costlier than keeping a current one.

- Closing a sale with a current customer is up to 14 times higher than that of closing a sale with a new one.

- 73% of satisfied customers are more likely to recommend a brand to others.

- 46% of satisfied customers will trust the existing brand's products over others.

- 5% increase in customer retention can increase profitability by up to 75%

- On average, loyal customers are up to 10 times as worth as during their first purchase.

- Lifetime value of a referred customer is 16% higher than that of a non-referred customer.

Thus, retaining customers is cheaper than acquiring new ones. However, what you must not forget that even the retained ones were once acquired. Hence, as you endeavor to retain existing customers, you must not sacrifice acquisition of new ones.

Customer retention strategy

Strategy 1: Create customer loyalty

Strategy 2: Improve customer support

Strategy 3: Create engaging content

Strategy 4: Build social community

Strategy 5: Listen to the voices of your customer

Strategy 6: Get back your lost customers

Getting back your lost customers

The following are steps win back your lost customers:

1. Politely and humbly ask them why they left.

2. Prove you are ready and willing to address their concerns.

3. Incentivize their return – Offer them a thank you gift for responding to you. Return incentives such as discount, bonus and related gifts.

4. Provide social proof – Tactically refer your customer to other customers who have been impressed with the turn-around.

5. Be genuinely helpful.

Steps in user retention:

1. Check how many users are returning

2. Find out why users are returning

3. Establish what users who are not returning missed that those who are returning got. This way, you can you can find a way to encourage them to return.

4. Create missing features that caused some users not to return.

Create customer loyalty

There are several ways to create customer loyalty. The following are some of them:

- Thank your customers for their purchase

- Reward customers for their purchase

- Deliver more than expected

CONCLUSION

Thank you for acquiring and reading this unique guide: "Growth Hacking: Innovative Marketing Tactics to Grow Faster and Smarter".

This book provides practical proven marketing tactics that you can easily apply to your business to grow faster and smarter. Many people have applied these tactics to achieve momentous growth rates. You too can be successful.

I hope you have endeavored to apply these tactics to propel your business growth rates. I also hope that you have recommended this guide to your friends and loved ones so that they too can uplift their business growth to greater heights.

Again, thank you for acquiring and reading this book.

Good luck!

The end… almost!

Reviews are not easy to come by.

As an independent author with a tiny marketing budget, I rely on readers, like you, to leave a short review on Amazon.

Even if it's just a sentence or two!

So if you enjoyed the book, please head to the product page, and leave a review as shown below.

I am very appreciative for your review as it truly makes a difference. Thank you from the bottom of my heart for purchasing this book and reading it to the end.